PARABLES FROM NATURE

PARABLES

The Parables of Jesus retold
for Young People

Illustrated

A companion book by the same author—
BIRD LIFE IN WINGTON

FROM NATURE

by John Calvin Reid

by Macy Schwarz

Wm. B. Eerdmans Publishing Co., Grand Rapids, Michigan

First Printed, 1954
Reprinted, February 1979

ISBN 0-8028-4025-6

PHOTOLITHOPRINTED BY EERDMANS PRINTING COMPANY
GRAND RAPIDS, MICHIGAN, UNITED STATES OF AMERICA

A Note About This Book

In the chancel of the Mt. Lebanon Presbyterian Church of Pittsburgh, Pennsylvania, is a glorious stained-glass window. In the very center the artist has portrayed the familiar and precious scene described by Mark in the tenth chapter of his Gospel, verses thirteen through sixteen:

"And they were bringing children to him, that he might touch them; and the disciples rebuked them. But when Jesus saw it he was indignant, and said to them, 'Let the children come to me, do not hinder them; for to such belongs the kingdom of God. Truly, I say to you, whosoever does not receive the kingdom of God like a child shall not enter it.' And he took them in his arms and blessed them, laying his hands upon them."

In a flash it came upon me, one day as I meditated in front of this window, that one of the reasons little children enjoyed being in the company of Jesus, no doubt, was that He told them stories.

5

What wonderful stories they must have been! How we wish the Gospel writers had preserved some of them!

Since they did not, why shouldn't someone undertake to retell and to interpret on a child's level the ones told to grown-ups, known as "The Parables," which have been preserved?

This little book is my humble effort to supply this need. It is published with the hope and prayer that through its pages the Saviour may continue to speak to and bless little children whose devoted parents and teachers are still bringing them to His loving arms.

— THE AUTHOR

CONTENTS

A Note About This Book 5

List of Illustrations 8

1. Nutty About Nuts 9
   *The Story of a Rich Man Who Was Very
   Foolish* (Luke 12:13-21) 13

2. Little Lost Lamb 16
   The Story of the Good Shepherd
   (Luke 15:1-7) 20

3. As Busy As a Bee 23
   *The Story of the Wise and Foolish Brides-
   maids* (Matthew 25:1-13) 28

4. How the Flowers Grow 31
   The Story of the Four Kinds of Soil
   (Matthew 13:1-8, 18-23) 35

5. Rebuilding Birch-View Dam 38
   The Story of Three Kinds of Workers
   (Matthew 20:1-16) 43

6. Mr. and Mrs. Wren's Second House 46
   The Story of Two Builders (Luke 6:46-49) 51

7. Corky Crow Tries a New Racket 53
   The Story of the King's Marriage Feast
   (Matthew 22:1-14) 57

8. Boulder Dam 60
   The Story of the Selfish Vineyard-Keepers
   (Luke 20:9-16) 64

9. School Days in the Ocean   67
   The Story of Three Men and Their Talents
      (Matthew 25:14-29)   71

10. The Fairy Magical Ring   75
   The Story of the Wheat and the Weeds
      (Matthew 13:24-30)   79

11. Man's Best Friend   82
   The Story of the Loving Father
      (Luke 15:11-24)   86

LIST OF ILLUSTRATIONS

1. Bushy was nutty about nuts   12

2. Every night Judy tucked Bootsie under the covers beside her   17

3. It was the coldest winter the bees had ever known   25

4. A lonely little petunia in an onion patch   34

5. They began to build the dam   42

6. It doesn't look as classy, but it is stronger   49

7. It was almost the end of Corky   56

8. Chief Swindle, the bandit chieftain   62

9. They wished for a place where they could sleep most of the time   69

10. The meeting of the Magical Ring   77

11. Man's best friend   85

PARABLE 1

Nutty About Nuts

Bushy Squirrel learned his lesson the hard way. Now he doesn't have any nuts at all — unless perhaps he may be able to borrow a few somewhere to take care of him through the rest of the winter.

But who would want to loan nuts to Bushy, since he was so selfish about his own supply?

And who would have thought, of all the Squirrels in the world, that Bushy would ever run short of nuts? There was a time when he had more than any other Squirrel in the forest.

I do not know when Bushy started being selfish. Probably it was when he was quite little. At any rate, by the time he was grown he was just nutty about nuts!

Of course, it was quite all right for him to store up a supply for the winter — all the Squirrels did that. But Bushy stored up three or four times as many as he needed for himself. Yet never would he give any to the Animal Chest, the Red Cross, or the Squirrel Scouts; or if he did, it would be only a few small ones that were partly spoiled.

Bushy was what some Squirrels called, "A Loan Shark." That is, he would loan nuts out at a very high rate of interest — twenty to a customer to be paid back next year, with ten extra as interest. So his supply grew and grew from year to year until he just didn't have room for all his nuts. Every hollow place in his tree was crammed full, and still he wasn't satisfied.

"Next year I must find a bigger tree in which to store my nuts," he said to himself. And so he did — a great hickory tree down beside the lake. Bushy found the big hollow place inside by walking right through the door which Mr. and Mrs. Woody Woodpecker had drilled in the tree. They were out gathering straw to build their nest at the time.

When they returned, Bushy had taken over. Not only did he drive out the Woodpeckers from the inside but he claimed the outside as well. He would not allow any other Squirrels to gather nuts from his tree and even be-

10

came angry at the Birds who only wanted to sit in the cool shade of the branches and sing.

"You might shake down some of the nuts," he barked, and drove them away.

So by the time winter came, Bushy had his big tree crammed full of nuts — many, many more than he needed.

"Take it easy," he said to himself when the wind began to howl and the snow to fall. "Take it easy, Bushy, and enjoy yourself. You have enough nuts laid up for several winters. Other Squirrels may be hungry and cold, but not you."

So he curled himself up on his big pile of nuts and went to sleep. Thus he did not know that the wind was blowing stronger and harder, and it never occurred to him that the trunk of his big hickory tree was quite weak because of the great hollow place where his nuts were stored.

He was dreaming peacefully about collecting more nuts next year when suddenly he was wakened by the harsh sound of breaking wood and the feeling that he was falling. The next moment there was a terrific splash! As Bushy inside his tree landed in the lake, the water came rushing in through the door and

Bushy was nutty about nuts

the nuts began pouring out at the same time.

Well, that's about all, except it was a Squirrel Scout that rescued Bushy from the lake; it was a Red Cross ambulance that rushed him to the hospital; and the ward to which he was taken was provided by the Animal Chest.

As I said at the beginning, maybe Bushy will be able to borrow enough nuts to keep him alive through the rest of the winter. But unless he remembers never, never to be selfish and greedy again, and instead to be helpful and kind by sharing with others, it might have been better if that Squirrel Scout had left him and all his nuts at the bottom of the lake!

The Story of a Rich Man Who Was Very Foolish
(Luke 12:13-21)

One day Jesus was teaching a great crowd of people who had come together to hear Him. After He had finished, a man came up to Him and said: "Teacher, tell my brother to divide with me the property which our father left us."

But Jesus refused to be drawn into their

selfish quarrel. "I am not a judge or a divider of property," He said.

After the man had gone his way, Jesus turned to His disciples who had heard the conversation and said: "Watch yourselves and stay away from selfishness; for life is not measured by how much a man has."

Then, to illustrate His meaning, He told them this story:

The land of a certain wealthy man was very rich and brought forth such a large harvest that the man said: "What will I do, for I do not have enough room to store my crops?"

It did not occur to him to give some to the poor, nor did he thank God for his good fortune. Instead he said to himself: "This I will do — I will tear down my old barns and build bigger ones, and then I will have room for my grain and my goods. And I will say to my soul, 'Soul, you have plenty of goods stored up for many years; take it easy, eat, drink, and have a good time.' "

But God was much displeased because the man was thinking only of himself. And God said to him, "You are a very foolish man. To-night your life comes to its end. After you are gone, whose will these things be that you call yours?"

By this story Jesus was teaching that in the sight of God true wealth consists not in what a man gets, but in what he gives.

PARABLE 2

Little Lost Lamb

Judy did not know Bootsie was lost until she went upstairs to get ready for bed. Bootsie was Judy's favorite doll. She had several others that were much prettier and two that were quite new, but for some strange reason she liked Bootsie best of all.

Bootsie was a fleecy little lamb with soft white wool all over. Every night for several years Judy had tucked Bootsie under the covers beside her and pulled his soft little body against her cheek before she went to sleep. But tonight she couldn't find him.

"Mother, have you seen Bootsie?" Judy called down the stairs, as she started to undress.

"Did you look under the bed?" her mother answered. "He must be somewhere in your room."

But he wasn't. Judy's mother came up-

Every night Judy tucked Bootsie under the covers beside her

stairs to help in the search, but they couldn't find Bootsie anywhere.

"Judy," said her mother, "you were up at Mrs. Garland's house this afternoon playing with Ann. Did you have Bootsie with you?"

"Oh, yes, Mother; I believe I did."

"Do you suppose you left Bootsie at Ann's house?" her mother asked.

Judy could not be sure, so her mother phoned Mrs. Garland.

"No," said Mrs. Garland, "Judy did not leave Bootsie here. I remember distinctly that she had him in her arms as she started home. She also had two story books and her roller skates. It was quite an armful. Do you suppose she dropped him on the way home?"

"Judy," said her mother, after she had finished talking with Mrs. Garland, "can't you sleep with one of your other dolls tonight? We will see if we can find Bootsie in the morning."

Just then Judy heard the sound of rain on the roof, and the tears came to her eyes.

"Oh, Mother," she said, "if I lost Bootsie on the way home, then he's out there in the rain. He'll get cold and wet. Please let us go find him. I can't go to sleep without my Bootsie."

Then Judy's mother did a very wonderful thing.

"If you love Bootsie that much," she said, "we will go try to find him."

A few minutes later, with raincoats, over-shoes, umbrella, and flashlight, they started out in the rain to look for Bootsie.

"Judy," her mother said, "you try to re-member exactly which way you walked home from Mrs. Garland's."

"I came the short way down the hill through Mrs. Garland's back yard," said Judy.

So together they walked up the hill in the direction of Mrs. Garland's house, toward her back yard. About halfway up, beside a rose-bush, they found Bootsie. Judy all but cried for joy as she gathered her little lamb into her arms.

Back home a few minutes later, she care-fully wiped the cold rain from Bootsie with a towel, wrapped him in a nice warm blanket, then tucked him under the cover in the bed beside her.

Judy's mother sat on the side of the bed as Judy said her good-night prayer:

"Now I lay me down to sleep,
I pray thee, Lord, my soul to keep;
Thy love go with me through the night,
And wake me with the morning light."

As Judy finished she said, "Wait, Mother, there's something else I want to say: 'Dear God, thank You for helping me to find Bootsie.'"

I am sure God must have been pleased with that prayer of Judy's, because you see, He loves little children — and grown-up people too — just as truly and even more tenderly than Judy loved her little lamb.

The Story of the Good Shepherd
(Luke 15:1-7)

In the time of Jesus there were a great many men who made their living by raising sheep.

But there were no fences in the pastures, and good grazing land was scarce. Often a shepherd would have to tend his flock many miles away from his home to find grass for his sheep, and sometimes one might fall behind or wander away and be lost from the flock. Each night the sheep were kept in a place called a "fold" — a walled-in space where they would be safe from wolves and robbers.

One day Jesus told the following story to the people who had come together to hear Him teach.

There was once a shepherd who had a hundred sheep. One night as he brought them into the fold he missed one. Quickly he counted them again. Yes, there were only ninety-nine.

Calling his son, who often helped him tend the sheep, he told him to keep a careful watch over those who were already in the fold, and he himself started back to hunt for the lost sheep. It was a long journey back to the valley where the sheep had been grazing that afternoon. It was growing dark. Robbers and wild beasts might be lurking along the way.

None of these things mattered to the shepherd. He was thinking only of his lost sheep. Could it have fallen into a pit? Perhaps its leg would be broken. He hoped and prayed that the wolves would not find it before he did.

Troubled by these thoughts, he hurried on. Ever so often he would pause, and over the hills his voice would roll, calling his sheep.

At last an answer came, a pitiful bleat from the distance in front of him.

The shepherd ran the rest of the way, guided by the bleating sounds that became clearer and clearer as he came closer. Yes, the lost sheep had fallen into a pit but, except for a few scratches from rocks and briars, it was unharmed.

Gently the shepherd lifted it to his shoulder. All the way back he carried it, his heart bursting with joy and gratitude because he had found it safe and sound.

Back home he rubbed oil into the wounds made by the rocks and briars; then he put the rescued sheep into the fold with the others.

But before he went to bed that night he called in his friends and neighbors to tell them what had happened. "It meant so much to me to find my sheep that was lost," he said, "that I wanted you to know about it and to share in my joy."

Jesus told this story to teach that God loves and cares for each one of us as this good shepherd loved and cared for his sheep.

PARABLE 3

As Busy As a Bee

This is the story of two colonies of Bees that settled not more than a mile apart, near a lovely flower-covered meadow in New England, known to the Bees as Honey-Land.

One was Bumble-Bee Colony, which had just flown up from Mexico, and the other was Honey-Bee Colony, which had lived in New England for some time.

Carlotta was the name of the queen who ruled over the Bumble-Bees, while the queen of the Honey-Bees was named Minerva.

About a week after Carlotta arrived, Minerva gave her a "buzz" and invited her to come over for tea. Carlotta was just a little surprised to find such hospitality and accepted with pleasure.

Between sips of tea and bites of honey sandwiches, the two queens chatted away and were

23

soon quite friendly. Minerva was mildly shocked when Carlotta told her that she and her colony had moved into the deserted nest of a field mouse and intended to make this their permanent home.

"But in the winter," said Minerva, "the ground will freeze, the snow will blow into your house, you will be very cold. You would be wise to find a hollow tree such as we have here."

"Too much trouble," replied Carlotta. "We Bumble-Bees believe in taking life easy. Besides, the ground will be cooler in the summer. My, but this is delicious honey," she said, wishing to change the subject. "Where did you get it?"

"It is left over from last winter," replied Minerva. "Our winters are quite severe up here, you know, so we always gather an extra supply just in case the cold should last longer than we expect. Last winter the weather was unusually mild. That explains why we still have a little old honey left. My bees are already busy gathering and storing up a supply for next winter."

It was the coldest winter the bees had ever known

"But it's only the first of April," said Carlotta. "I do not see any use in starting to work so soon. There are five full months left before it will begin to get cold."

As you may have guessed, the two colonies of Bees were just like their queens.

The Honey-Bees worked from dawn until dark, flying far and wide over the meadow and even beyond it to find and bring home their baskets of honey to feed their babies and to store up an extra supply for winter.

The Bumble-Bees worked only when they felt like it. As long as there was plenty of clover in the meadow, they did bring in enough honey for themselves and their babies, so that no one was hungry during the spring and summer. But they did not believe the stories they heard about the cold winters in New England, so they did not bother very much about providing an extra winter supply.

Winter soon came, and, as it happened, it was the coldest winter even the Honey-Bees had ever known. By Christmas they were rationing one-half the usual amount in the hope that they could have enough to last until the new flowers should appear.

It was in January that five Bumble-Bees knocked at their door to bring an urgent plea from their queen: "Please send us some of your honey; ours is almost gone."

"I am very sorry, but we cannot," answered Queen Minerva, when the Bumble-Bees were shown into her presence. "Already our own Bees are going hungry each day trying to make our supply last until spring. We do not have enough to loan or sell lest our own children should starve."

Some of the Honey-Bees did die before spring arrived — so cold was the winter and so long. But several thousand lived and as soon as the flowers began to bloom again, they and their new children, hatched from the new eggs of their queen, started out again, searching for honey and bringing it in, basketful after basketful, more determined than ever to have a full supply for their next winter's needs.

As for the Bumble-Bees, not one Bee lived through that dreadful winter except Queen Carlotta. She learned too late the lesson Queen Minerva tried to teach her at her April tea party!

The Story of the Wise and Foolish Bridesmaids

(Matthew 25:1-13)

In every country in the world weddings have always been gay and happy occasions.

In the land and time of Jesus, weddings usually took place at night and were followed by a big supper, or reception, called the wedding feast. It was also the custom for the best friends of the groom to go out to meet him and to return with him with joyous singing and laughter to the place where the wedding and the feast were to be.

Each guest was supposed to carry a lighted lamp as a sign of welcome and to help light the path along which the wedding party was to travel.

The kingdom of heaven, Jesus once said, is like a wedding in which ten bridesmaids went out with their lamps to meet the bridegroom. Five of them were foolish and five were wise.

The foolish took no extra oil. There was oil in their lamps. They thought that would be enough, so that was all they took.

But the wise each carried a flask of oil in addition to the oil that was in their lamps.

They did not know they would need it, but they brought along the extra oil anyway.

It so happened that the bridegroom was much later than anyone expected. As a matter of fact, he did not arrive until midnight. By that time the bridesmaids were all dozing by the roadside.

All of a sudden someone cried, "The bridegroom is coming. It is time to go to meet him!"

Hurriedly the ten bridesmaids began to prepare their lamps. By this time the oil in each was almost all used up. The five wise maidens began to refill their lamps from the flasks they had brought with them and to trim their wicks.

The five foolish maidens were very much distressed. "Give us some of your oil," they pleaded, "for our lamps are about to go out."

"We cannot," the wise replied, "we only brought enough to refill our lamps. Perhaps you can find a storekeeper who will sell you some."

The five foolish maidens rushed away to buy, and while they were gone the bridegroom arrived. Those who were ready joined

29

his party and went on with him to the mar
riage feast, and the door was shut.

After a while the foolish maidens arrived.
But by this time it was too late. The feast had
already begun and the doorkeeper would not
let them in. Thus they missed the marriage
supper.

By this story Jesus was teaching how important it is to be well prepared at all times.

PARABLE 4

How the Flowers Grow

Four little Petunia seeds, nestling close to their mother's heart, under her soft pink petals, dreamed of the day when they would grow up to be beautiful flowers like their mother.

One of the four, whose name was Constance, listened very attentively as their mother said to them: "The time will soon come, my dear children, when you must go forth to seek and to find a home of your own. Some parts of the earth are hard like stone and brick; there no plants can grow. Other parts are filled with weeds and thorns; there you would not be able to find room to grow. But other parts are warm and soft, and there flowers find it easy to grow."

She went on to tell them more about the soil under her own roots: how it was prepared by a lovely lady who was very fond of flowers; how the lady chopped the soil with her hoe to make it soft, and mixed in fertilizer to

31

make it rich; how she planted her flower seeds with great care; how after they began to grow she would come out with her water pail to give them a drink when they were thirsty; and how she would dig gently around their roots so the warmth of the sun could get in.

"That explains," said the mother of the little Petunia seeds, "why my petals are so pink and my stem so strong. And now you understand why I want each of you to grow up in the same rich soil that has been so kind to me."

"Mother," said Constance, "how can we be sure to be planted in this soft, warm soil bed about which you have told us?"

"Whatever you do," their mother replied, "beware of the Wind. He may come some night and invite you to go for a ride in his airplane. You must never, never go to ride with the Wind."

Sure enough, one night the Wind did come whizzing around the corner. "Come, go for a ride with me," he called to the little Petunia seeds. "We will see the world together, whee!"

Now three of the little seeds decided to go with the wind. They had not listened very carefully to what their mother had said. Besides, they felt she did not always know what was best for them.

"What fun to go for a ride on the wings of the Wind," they thought, so away they flew.

The Wind dropped one of them on a street pavement some distance away. The pavement was cold and hard, and the next morning a tiny finch found it and ate it up.

Another fell in a crack between two bricks in the street where there was a little soil. It sprouted and grew for a few days; then it withered and died under the heat of the sun.

A third seed fell in the midst of some wild onions. After it had sprouted, the onions crowded in close so that the little Petunia had little chance to grow. It became very, very unhappy. Over and over again it sang a sad little song:

"I'm a lonely little Petunia in an onion patch,
An onion patch, an onion patch,
And all I do is cry all day,
Boohoo, Boohoo,
The air's so bad it takes my breath away."

But Constance refused to go to ride with the Wind. Instead, she nestled closer than ever to her mother's heart.

Then one night when the rain was falling

A lonely little petunia in an onion patch

gently, she slipped out of her pod and dropped down into the soil just under her mother's stem.

Before long the litle seed was a sprout, then a plant, growing larger and larger every day. The lovely lady who took such good care of her flower garden came with her pail to give Constance a drink of water. All during the spring she cared for the new little Petunia, just as she had done the year before for her mother.

Thus it came to pass that Constance became one of the sweetest and most beautiful flowers in the lady's garden. She had children of her own now — several little Petunia seeds under the petals of her lovely bloom. Let us hope that all of them will be wise like their mother and plant themselves in the soft, rich soil under her roots.

The Story of the Four Kinds of Soil
(Matthew 13:1-8, 18-23)

One day Jesus was teaching by the side of the Lake of Galilee. As the crowd increased, many were not able to see or to hear Him. So He entered into a boat, rowed a little way out into the lake, and from that point taught the people as they stood along the shore.

Jesus knew that some of them were deeply interested in what He was saying, while others were there only because of curiosity, so He told them this story.

There was once a farmer who went out to sow his seed. As he walked across his field, scattering the grain far and wide, some seeds fell upon a path by the side of the field, and later the birds came and gobbled them up.

Other seeds fell among the rocks, where there was not much soil. These seeds sprouted and tried to grow, but because there was so little soil for their roots, they withered away and died under the hot sun.

Still other seeds fell in a weed-and-briar patch. These, too, tried to grow, but the weeds and briars grew faster and choked out the good seeds.

But there were some seeds that fell in the good, soft soil of the farmer's field. These sprang up and grew and brought forth a wonderful harvest. Some stalks produced a hundred grains, some produced sixty, and others produced thirty.

Later Jesus explained to His disciples what He meant by this story.

When one hears the Word of God without trying to understand, he soon forgets what he has heard. The seeds of truth are snatched away from his mind, just as the seeds of grain that fell upon the wayside path were carried away by the birds.

Another person may hear the Word of God with joy and go his way intending to practice what he has heard. Later, when others laugh at him or call him sneering names, he loses his courage. Thus his good intentions weaken and die, as the grain among the rocks, where there was not much soil, withered under the hot sun.

Another person may listen with his mind full of other thoughts. He may be thinking about making more money and having a good time, or he may be worrying about what may happen tomorrow. So the Word of God finds no place in his heart. It is choked out like the seeds of grain that fell among the weeds.

But there is another kind of person — one who listens, who wants to understand, and tries to practice what he hears. Such a person's life pleases God just as the fruitful grain growing in the good soil pleases the farmer.

PARABLE 5

Rebuilding Birch-View Dam

The storm was terrific — a cloudburst in fact, although the Beavers in Birch-View Colony did not know enough about the various kinds of storms to call it by that name.

But one thing they did know when daylight dawned the next morning. There was a wide break in the dam they had built just below their house. The water was pouring through it at such a rate that they realized it would have to be repaired that very day or else their lake would drain dry.

Bruso, their chief, was the most respected of all the Beavers in Beaver County. He was known everywhere for his justice and wisdom.

"We will begin work at once," said he to Willie Webfoot, who happened to be the best swimmer in his colony. "But we will have to have extra workers if we are to finish before dark. You swim downstream as fast as you can and ask some other Beavers from the colonies down the river to come up and help us."

Willie dived in gracefully and was soon out of sight.

The first Beavers to whom he told his story did not seem very much concerned. "How much does Chief Bruso pay?" asked one of them, still stretched out in the warm sun.

"Listen," said Willie earnestly, "all of you know that Chief Bruso is always kind and fair. He did not tell me how much he would pay, but it is very important that our dam be repaired today. Will you please come and help?"

Six of the Beavers to whom he had been talking decided they would at least go up and see the break in the dam. On the way they agreed that they would not work without a contract, and one of their number was appointed to talk with Chief Bruso.

So, when they arrived, their leader went over to where Chief Bruso was directing the work. "How much do you pay?" he asked. "We cannot work for nothing, you know."

Chief Bruso was frankly surprised. He himself was so generous and unselfish that he could not understand these Beavers who made the matter of pay so important. But he kept his thoughts to himself.

"I will pay each one of you five pieces of fresh birch bark if you will work from now until sundown."

"Make it six pieces," said their leader, "and we'll do it."

"All right," said Bruso, knowing he could not afford to lose time in arguing.

About noon another colony of Beavers, sent by Willie, arrived from down the river. While they did not ask outright how much they would be paid, they did wait for Chief Bruso to make them an offer.

He realized what they were thinking and said, "If you will help, I will pay you whatever is right. We must hurry if we are to finish before dark."

With that promise they also jumped in and began to work.

Later that afternoon another colony of Beavers arrived. Willie Webfoot was with them. When he told them about Chief Bruso's trouble, they asked no questions but immediately said to Willie, "Of course, we will go and help to rebuild the dam!"

And now, having arrived, they still asked

40

no questions. Although tired from their long swim up the stream, they dived right in and began dragging logs and sticks into place and sealing them with mud.

And so it was that by sundown the dam was finished, and Chief Bruso called all the visiting Beavers over to a big pile of birch bark to give them their pay.

First he called for those who had arrived last. To each Beaver he gave six pieces of fresh birch bark. Then he turned to those who had arrived around noon. To each of these he gave also six pieces of bark. Then came those who had arrived early in the morning. They expected that they would receive more, but to each of them Chief Bruso gave also six pieces of bark.

The early workers then began to grumble and complain. "But we worked all day in the boiling sun. These who came last worked only about an hour in the cool of the afternoon."

Chief Bruso fastened a stern eye upon them. "You made an agreement, didn't you?" he said. "You refused to work without a contract. Then, take what you bargained for and be gone. These Beavers who came last asked

They began to build the dam

no questions. They were willing to work simply because they saw I needed them. Therefore I will pay them as much as I did you."

When this story became known throughout Beaver County, all the Beavers knew that to Chief Bruso it mattered not simply how long a Beaver worked or how much he did, but much more in what spirit he did his work. And he became even more famous for his justice and wisdom.

The Story of Three Kinds of Workers
(Matthew 20:1-16)

One day Jesus told His disciples this story.

Once there was a landowner who went out early in the morning to hire men to work in his vineyard. The first group he hired wanted a definite agreement. He promised to pay them five dollars a day, and sent them into his vineyard.

About nine o'clock he found another group of men and asked them to work for him. "I will pay you what is right," he said. So they also went into the vineyard. He did the same thing at noon and at three o'clock.

About five o'clock he found another group standing idle. "Would you like to work in my vineyard?" he asked. This group went in and began to work without any promise at all.

At the close of the day the landowner said to the foreman in charge of his vineyard: "Call the workmen and pay them their wages. Pay first those who started to work last."

When those who had started to work at five o'clock came, each man received five dollars. When those who had been hired at the beginning of the day came, they thought they would receive more. But they, too, were paid five dollars each.

Then they began to grumble at the owner of the vineyard. "These men who came in at five o'clock," they said, "worked only one hour. And you have made their wages equal to ours, who have worked all day under the hot sun."

But the landowner replied to the one who had spoken: "My friend, I am not being unfair to you. You made an agreement with me for five dollars a day, and that is what you have been paid. If I choose to be generous to those who trusted me and were willing to work without an agreement, is it any affair

44

of yours? Do I not have a right to do what I will with what belongs to me? You have received the amount you asked for; take it and go home."

By this story Jesus was teaching that we should serve God with a glad and willing heart, because the spirit in which we work counts more with Him than the amount of work we do.

PARABLE 6

Mr. and Mrs. Wren's Second House

Fortunately Mr. Wren was not very far away. When he heard the crash, he hurried home as fast as his wings could carry him. There at the foot of the tree lay their pretty little house, but Mrs. Wren was not to be seen anywhere.

"Margie, Margie!" he called. "Where are you?"

From inside the house he heard a faint chirp. Rushing in, he found Mrs. Wren dazed and frightened, but not seriously hurt.

"I think I'm all right," she said. "Help me out, so I can get some fresh air."

From the outside Mr. and Mrs. Wren surveyed their wrecked house and wondered what to do. They had chosen it early in the spring because it was so new and pretty. Built by a Boy Scout, it had four plank walls and a floor, an arched roof, a neat round front door, and a fresh coat of grey paint.

The bottom plank was nailed about fifteen feet above the ground to the trunk of a wild cherry tree. Mr. and Mrs. Wren had been so thrilled with the looks of the little house that they had failed to notice the split in the floor plank where it was nailed to the tree. Merrily they had moved in and begun building their nest. Before long their work was completed, and Mrs. Wren had already laid one egg when the wind storm came that widened the split in the weak plank until it broke in two; and their house, nest, egg, Mrs. Wren and all, came tumbling to the ground.

"We should have noticed how poorly it was fastened to the tree," said Mrs. Wren. "Never again will we choose a house simply because it looks nice from the outside."

So Mr. and Mrs. Wren began looking around for a place to build a second nest, and what kind of house do you suppose they chose this time? Believe it or not, the mailbox on the front of Mr. Mann's brick house!

As a matter of fact, they had a chance to go back to their pretty little grey wooden house, for within a few hours after it had fallen, the Boy Scout nailed it together again and put it back in the same wild cherry tree. This time he fastened it very carefully with a strong wire. Mr. and Mrs. Wren looked it over, but decided upon the mailbox instead.

"This house," said Mrs. Wren to her husband, "is not pretty like the little grey wooden house. Its shape is square, its roof flat, its color black, and it is rusty in spots — but it is made of metal and securely fastened by two strong screws to the porch wall. It doesn't look as classy as the other house, but it is stronger and more secure. Here our children will be safe no matter how hard the rain falls or how strong the wind blows."

Now when Mr. Mann noticed that the Wrens were building their nest in his mailbox, he watched for the mailman and, as soon as he saw him coming, told him to please leave the mail each morning on the inside of the front screen door so that the Wrens could have the exclusive use of the mailbox for their new home.

Before summer arrived, there were three little eggs in the Wrens' nest; and before summer was ended, the three little eggs had become three little Wrens.

When finally they were strong enough to fly away with their father and mother and to

It doesn't look as classy, but it is stronger

add their merry songs to the music of Bird Land, Mr. and Mrs. Wren were very happy, and Mrs. Wren said, "What a wonderful home that was in which to raise our children! How fortunate we were to find such a strong, safe house!"

"Yes," replied Mr. Wren, "and how kind Mr. Mann and the mailman were to allow us to have it rent-free. What do you say that we go back next year and see if we can make the same arrangements?"

To this Mrs. Wren heartily agreed. I feel sure that Mr. Mann and the mailman will both be glad to see them again, don't you?

And now I want to tell you something special. Almost all of the story about Mr. and Mrs. Wren is true. One spring two wrens built their first nest in a Boy Scout birdhouse near my home. Then the house fell down. And then those two wrens built their nest and raised their little family in my mailbox! Only a short time before Mr. and Mrs. Wren moved in, I had written a book about birds, and now a family of birds was living right in my mailbox. Maybe they had read the book. It is for children and is called *Bird Life in Wington.*

The Story of Two Builders
(Luke 6:46-49)

When Jesus was here upon the earth, there were a great many people who followed Him, hoping to receive the good things He was able to give, but who were very careless about obeying Him.

As He said, they were always calling Him their Master, but did not do the things He taught.

To warn them against this, one day He told them a story about two men who were planning to build a house.

The first man was very careful about everything. He selected rock for the foundation of his house. He used only the best of materials and saw to it that all parts were fastened together firmly.

The second man used the earth for his foundation, bought cheap materials, and was very careless about how the parts were nailed together. His house looked very well from the outside, but the real test came one day when a great storm blew up. Close to both houses was a stream that overflowed its banks.

Rushing against the house that was poorly

built, the stream began to wash away its earth foundation, and before long the walls caved in with a mighty crash. The house was completely ruined.

The same rain and wind beat down upon the other house. The same stream rushed against its sides. But since this house was so strongly built and had rock for its foundation, the stream did not even shake it. It was just as secure after the storm as before.

People who hear His words and do them, Jesus said, are like the man who built the strong house. But people who are not careful to obey are like the man who built the weak house that was destroyed by the storm!

PARABLE 7

Corky Crow Tries a New Racket

As Corky Crow sat on top of the tree, picking shot out of his leg, he thought he saw a new way to get something for nothing.

His old way had become rather dangerous. Stealing corn had been fun at first, but dodging Mr. Farmer's buckshot was anything but fun, as the sore place on his leg reminded him.

Down in the park below, the pigeons were having their dinner. Every day a kind old lady took her seat on a bench there beside the sidewalk and fed them from her hand.

"What a nice, easy way to make a living," said Corky, as he watched them. "Wonder how I would look in a new grey suit? Not bad, not bad!" And away he flew to his tailor!

A week later, at noon, he was down in the park with the pigeons, eating the crumbs and peanuts and popcorn that the kind old lady scattered at her feet or held out in her hand.

In his new grey suit, Corky looked so much like a pigeon that not even the old lady noticed that he wasn't a pigeon.

The pigeons were so contented and happy that every now and then they would say "Thank you" to the kind lady. In pigeon language this sounded like "Coo, Coo."

Now Corky did not know what "Coo, Coo" meant. He thought it meant "More, More," so, moving in close to the old lady, he said, "Caw, Caw!"

When they heard that, all the pigeons stopped both their cooing and eating, and looked in astonishment at Corky!

"Who ever heard a pigeon say 'Caw'?" exclaimed one.

"It's Corky Crow," shouted another. "Last month he stole three eggs from my nest."

In a flash they all rushed at him and perhaps would have pecked every feather out of his new suit had Corky not been so quick on the wing. He saw what was coming and darted away, with every pigeon in the flock after him. Fortunately for Corky, he had stronger wings than they, so he made his escape into a nearby forest.

Alighting at last on a limb to catch his

breath, he said to himself, "If I had only kept my big mouth shut!"

And the next time he did. By which I mean Corky Crow did not give up easily. He liked being fed in the park; and a week later, with his new gray suit freshly cleaned and pressed, he was back with the pigeons again, determined to let the pigeons do all the cooing this time.

Everything went fine until the old lady held out a handful of nuts to three of the little squab pigeons who were only about four months old. Corky Crow was about two feet away eating crumbs when he saw that handful of nuts and heard the lady's kind voice as she called to the three little squabs.

And what do you suppose he did? He hopped right over them and started eating the nuts himself! Once again all the pigeons turned and looked with astonishment at Corky.

"Whoever saw a pigeon hop?" said one. "A pigeon walks, a crow hops—it's Corky again!"

Before Corky knew what was happening, they were on him, pecking and scratching for all they were worth.

And that was the end of Corky's grey suit.

It was almost the end of Corky

It was almost the end of Corky, as a matter of fact, but he finally managed to get free from the flock of pigeons and back to his forest hide-out again. Only this time he left more feathers behind him than he carried away.

As Dr. Snowbird painted his scratches with cranberry juice a few hours later, he listened to Corky's story and then remarked dryly, "Corky, if you want to know the truth, the kind of change you need is a change of heart."

The Story of the King's Marriage Feast
(Matthew 22:1-14)

One day, while visiting with His disciples, Jesus said to them: "These things I have spoken to you that my joy may be in you, and that your joy may be full."

By this He meant that following Him ought to make people happy and never sad. It should put gladness into their hearts and smiles upon their faces.

Many of the stories Jesus told about the kingdom of God were intended to teach this same truth — that to be a Christian means joy and happiness. This is true of those stories in which Jesus compares God's kingdom to a wedding or a great supper.

One such story told by Jesus was this.

The kingdom of heaven may be compared to a king who gave a marriage feast for his son. A great many invitations were sent out in advance. Then later the king sent his servants to remind those that had been invited that the day of the feast had arrived.

Some who had been invited were very rude. They made silly excuses to the king's servants, laughed at them, and refused to come.

Then the king said to his servants: "The wedding feast will soon be ready. Go out into the streets and invite as many as you find. My house must be full tonight."

The servants did as the king commanded. Soon the wedding hall was filled with guests. It was a gay and happy time for all.

But when the king came to greet his guests, he noticed one man who was not dressed in a wedding robe, such as all the others were wearing.

There was no excuse for this, because, as the custom was in those days, the king provided from his own wardrobe wedding robes for all guests who might not have their own.

The king said to the man: "Friend, how

does it happen that you do not have on a wedding robe?"

The man stood speechless. He had insulted the king and his court, and had no excuse to offer. So the king told his servants to put the man outside.

Afterward, the wedding and the feast proceeded, being greatly enjoyed by all.

PARABLE 8

Boulder Dam

No king of Ant-ovia had ever been more kind and generous to his subjects than King Justus. By his order his land had been divided into ten equal parts and given over to ten groups of Ants known as colonies. Each colony organized its own government and was free to do as it pleased, except that, for the use of his land, King Justus required a certain amount of grain to be brought to him at the time of harvest each year.

For a while all went well in Ant-ovia. Then one colony, led by a bandit chieftain whose name was Swindle, rebelled and failed to send to King Justus his share of the harvest.

"Surely there must be some misunderstanding," said King Justus. "I will send a messenger to find out why I have not received my part of the grain."

Now Chief Swindle had built himself a

fortress down at the bottom of a narrow gorge beside a stream. At the entrance to the gorge he stationed guards to spread the alarm in case of attack. In the fortress an army of three thousand Ants was kept in readiness for battle.

When Swindle heard that the king was sending a messenger, he laughed in his cruel heart and said, "The old king must be getting soft. I had expected his army." Then he gave orders that his guards should seize the messenger at the entrance to the gorge, beat him, and send him back home. This same treatment was given to two other messengers sent later by the king.

"What shall I do?" Justus said to himself. "To think that my former subjects could be so selfish and cruel! Surely there is some way to reach their hearts by kindness. I know what I will do. I will send to them my only son whom I love best of all. Surely they will respect and listen to him, and he will be able to win back their loyalty."

When the hardhearted Swindle heard that the king's son was coming, he called for his army captains and said: "This is our big chance. Justus has only one son. If we get

Chief Swindle, the bandit chieftain

rid of him, then, when the old king dies, we can take over the whole kingdom." So they killed the king's son!

The king's heart was broken when he heard what had happened. "I will show patience no longer," he said, addressing the commander of his army. "Swindle and his rebels must be destroyed and their land given to other Ants who can be trusted."

"Sir," said the commander, "I have a plan already mapped out. By this time tomorrow not one of the rebel Ants will be left alive."

Now the commander had scouted the territory of the rebel Ants and had discovered on the edge of the gorge just above their fortress a rock about the shape and size of a football —which, of course, was a huge boulder as Ants measure size! It was quite a simple matter for the field engineers in the king's army to dig a tunnel under this boulder and to carry out several thousand grains of sand, one at a time, until the boulder tumbled over the side of the gorge and landed with a mighty crash right on top of Swindle's fort, grinding it to dust! Then, rolling on into the water, it dammed up the stream, thereby forming a lake that completely covered the city the rebel

Ants had built around the fortress of their wicked chief.

The beautiful waterfall at the lower end of the lake is known to this day as Boulder Dam. From all parts of Ant-ovia tourist Ants travel to see it. As they look at the great rock with the water splashing over it, they are reminded of what a wonderful ruler they have in King Justus, and of how wicked and foolish it was for the rebel Ants not to love and obey him.

The Story of the Selfish Vineyard-Keepers
(Luke 20:9-16)

How many times a day do you suppose you use the word "My" or "Mine"? You say, for example, "My eyes," "My hands," "My mind," "My money," "My clothes," and "My friends."

But are these things really yours? Jesus taught that the earth and everything in it belongs to God. He is the owner of all things. Everything we have is "loaned" or "rented" to us by Him. We should always remember this and be grateful, and also never fail to give God what He rightfully expects in return for these blessings and opportunities we have received from Him. These were some of the thoughts Jesus had in mind when He told the following story.

Once upon a time there was a man who owned a vineyard. He himself had planted the vines and had tended them for several years.

He also had business interests in another country, and in due time he decided to go into that country for a long visit.

But he did not sell his vineyard. He let it out to tenants with the understanding that they would give him a certain share of the grapes.

When the time for ripe grapes arrived, he sent a servant to receive his portion of the fruit of the vineyard.

The tenants beat the servant and sent him away without anything at all.

The owner of the vineyard, being a very patient man, sent a second servant. He, too, was beaten and sent away empty-handed.

Then he sent a third. He was treated even more shamefully than the other two, and given no fruit.

But the owner's patience was not yet exhausted. "What shall I do?" he said to himself. Then he decided to send his son whom he dearly loved. "Surely they will respect him," he said, "and share with him the fruit of the vineyard."

But, instead, those wicked tenants said, when they saw the owner's son coming, "This is the heir. The vineyard will be his when his father dies. But if we kill him, it will be ours."

So they seized him, dragged him out of the vineyard, and killed him.

What a terrible crime! The owner of the vineyard could hardly believe it when he heard what had been done. He had come to the end of his patience. He hurried back home to see that justice was done, and before long those wicked tenants received the same punishment that they had visited upon the owner's son.

Then the owner let out the vineyard to other tenants, who respected him, took good care of the vines, and gave to him, as owner, his rightful share of the fruit.

PARABLE 9

School Days in the Ocean

This is the story of two fish families who lived in the ocean. I shall call them "The Sluggards" and "The Hustlers."

Of course, there were other families of fish besides these two, but there was nothing unusual about the rest. They were and still are just ordinary fish such as you have seen many times in the fish market.

The Sluggards were very unhappy in the ocean. They didn't like to go to school or to do anything that called for hard work. They wanted life to be easy.

So, one day they swam out of the ocean up into a quiet little stream where there were no big waves to bother them or sea monsters to frighten them.

But the sunlight annoyed them. They wished for a dark, cool place where they could sleep most of the time and never be troubled about anything.

In the end they found it. They, or rather their children, now live in a stream known as "Echo River," which runs away down under the earth through the famous Mammoth Cave of Kentucky.

The most unusual thing about these fish, as you may know, is that they are blind. For so many years they have lived down under the earth, where they never use their eyes, that their eyes have gradually dried up and disappeared. Only two small wrinkles remain on the sides of their heads, where once were two bright round eyes.

The Hustlers were too industrious to be satisfied with a quiet easy life. They were determined to be something more than just ordinary fish in the ocean.

Some of them specialized in *physical education*. By exercising and stretching their muscles as they took their daily swimming lessons, they became larger and larger and also stronger until today some of them, such as the Giant Tuna, weigh as much as one thousand pounds and grow to be ten feet long or more.

Others specialized in *art*. Later they moved down to the tropical seas for graduate courses

They wished for a place where they could sleep
most of the time

in painting and decorating. Some of these have developed such a vivid variety of colors in the suits and coats they wear that they resemble butterflies and are called Butterfly Fish.

Others became interested in *electrical engineering* and learned how to make electricity in their own bodies. If a man were to touch an Electric Eel, for example, he would receive a shock just as if he had touched a live electric wire.

Others became interested in *singing* and moved to the West Coast of the United States to take voice lessons. They are known as the Singing Fish of California.

Still others became interested in *exploring*. The so-called Frog Fish have learned how to explore the bottom of the sea and have developed two fins shaped like feet with which they can walk on the floor of the ocean. In like manner, the Climbing Perch became interested in exploring the land; and upon the eastern coast of India, in damp weather, they crawl out on the land and sometimes climb the trunks of small trees, using the special "feet" which they have developed for this purpose.

Most unusual of all, some became interested in *flying*. They practiced flapping and spreading their fins again and again, until they became able to leap up out of the ocean and sail for quite a distance in the air.

Such are some of the amazing things the Hustlers have been able to accomplish by perseverance and hard work.

What a difference between them and the blind Sluggards in Echo River in Mammoth Cave! But they all started out in the same school!

The Story of Three Men and Their Talents
(Matthew 25:14-29)

Did you ever wonder why some people in the world have so many more opportunities and abilities than others? Jesus once told a story to teach that the important thing in God's eyes is not how many we have, but how we use the ones God has given us.

This is the story.

There was once a wealthy businessman who planned to take a trip to a country far away. He called his servants and turned over to them his property.

The amount he gave to the first was worth

around five thousand dollars; to the second he gave two thousand dollars; to the third, one thousand dollars. Then the man went away as he had planned.

The first servant, who had received five thousand dollars, got busy at once. He wisely used his money in buying and selling merchandise, and in time he made five thousand dollars more.

The second servant also wisely invested his two thousand dollars and made two thousand dollars more.

But the third servant was lazy. He made no effort at all to invest his one thousand dollars or to buy and sell with it and thus to make it increase. He simply hid it and kept it safe.

After a long time, the wealthy man returned from his journey and called his three servants to him to find out what they had done with his property and to settle accounts with them.

The first, who had received the five thousand dollars, came forward bringing ten thousand dollars. "Sir," he said, "you gave me five thousand dollars. I have made five thousand dollars more."

His master said to him: "You have done well and have been a good and faithful servant. You deserve and shall have a good promotion. And I want you to be my guest at a feast in my house tonight."

Then the servant who had received two thousand dollars came forward bringing four thousand dollars. "Sir, you gave me two thousand dollars," he said. "I have increased it to four thousand dollars."

"You, too, have done well," said his master, "and shall have a good promotion. You also are invited to the feast at my house tonight."

Then came the servant who had received the one thousand dollars. "Master," he said, "I knew you to be a hard man, reaping where you did not sow and taking what you did not work for. I was afraid of what you might do if I lost your money; so I went and hid it. Here is your one thousand dollars."

But his master answered him, "You have been wicked and very lazy. If you thought I was a hard man, then you should have been all the more careful to do what I expected and not to displease me. You should have invested my money so as to have made it increase."

Then he ordered the money to be taken from him and given to the servant who had done so well with the five thousand dollars.

Thus Jesus taught that those who do not use their abilities and opportunities will lose them, while those who use them well will receive more and more.

PARABLE 10

The Fairy Magical Ring

The meeting will come to order," said Queen Titania, as she took her place upon her throne, the largest mushroom in the Magical Ring. The other fairies found seats upon other mushrooms, and at last stopped their excited chattering. Several tiny hands were high in the air, signaling for permission to speak. Among them, Puck's was waving frantically.

"All right, Puck," said Titania, "you may speak first. Do you still have a pain in your tummy?"

"Yes, I do," answered Puck. "The doctor says it will be two or three days before I am completely well. I want to make a motion that we organize ourselves into a fairy army, using our wands as swords, and that we destroy every poisonous mushroom in the forest. How I hate those Amanitas!"

As you may know, the Amanita is one of the most beautiful of all the mushrooms. It has a delicate red umbrella top, set upon a graceful stem. But far from being good to eat, it is very poisonous.

That explained Puck's tummy-ache. The day before he had taken just one bite of an Amanita. Five minutes later he was deathly sick. Only the quick arrival of Titania and her magic wand had saved his life.

The majority of the fairies were in favor of Puck's motion. Twink reminded the Council that poisonous mushrooms were harmful to human beings as well as to fairies. "There was once a cruel Roman emperor by the name of Nero," he said, "who killed off a whole party of guests whom he did not like by feeding them poisonous mushrooms."

"Yes," agreed Blink, "and there was a famous Russian Czar named Alexis who died from eating Amanitas by mistake."

"Puck has the right idea," said Swink, the next fairy to speak. "As good fairies we owe it to the world of human beings, as well as to ourselves, to destroy all poisonous mushrooms. I call for a vote on his motion."

The meeting of the Magical Ring

"Just a minute," said Titania. "How about the good mushrooms? We do not want to destroy them, for then we would have no Magical Ring in which to meet for our Councils and to hold our parties. And there would be no more mushroom soup and no mushrooms to serve with sirloin steaks! If we set out to destroy all poisonous mushrooms, how can we tell the difference between them and those that are good to eat?"

"That is easy," said Puck, still thinking of his experience the day before. "The ones with tops like umbrellas are poisonous."

"Not all of them," answered Titania. "You are sitting on an umbrella. It is not an Amanita but a Dog Mushroom. It is quite delicious, and contains no poison whatsoever."

After some discussion, the fairies agreed that only an expert could be sure just which mushrooms were good to eat and which ones were poisonous. Then their queen reminded them of another thing. Often a poisonous mushroom might be found growing right beside others that were good. It would be impossible to destroy it without harming the others.

"I suppose I will have to withdraw my mo-

78

tion," said Puck, "but how much better life would be if there were no poisonous mushrooms!"

"Are you sure?" asked Titania quietly. "If all the mushrooms were good and if there were no evil things in the forest to keep us on our guard, then my fairies might become very careless and lazy. We might be better off if there were nothing evil and poisonous in the forest, but I do not think we would be better fairies."

At this point the Fairy Council agreed that the queen was right and the meeting adjourned. But before the fairies went home to bed, Queen Titania gave them for refreshments ice-cold mushroom punch served in buttercups and sweetened with honey.

The Story of the Wheat and the Weeds
(Matthew 13:24-30)

Did you ever ask yourself the question, "Why does God allow bad people to be in His world?" The people who are selfish and mean and hateful, who commit all the terrible crimes you read about in the newspapers — why doesn't He destroy them and leave in the world only those who are good?

But who are the good? All bad people have some good in them, and all good people have some evil in them. No one is altogether good, and no one is altogether bad.

Moreover, there is always the chance that the bad man may change his ways and become good. And a bad man may have a good father and mother who still love him and are hoping and praying that he will become a good man. They would be heartbroken if their son was destroyed while he was still wicked.

These are some of the reasons why God does not destroy bad people. Jesus was thinking of all this when He told the following story.

In managing His kingdom God may be said to be like a farmer who sowed good wheat in his field. But at night while he and his servants were asleep, an enemy came and sowed weeds in the same field where the farmer had sowed the wheat.

So when the plants came up, the weeds appeared also.

The servants of the farmer came to him and said, "Sir, did you not sow good seed in your field? How then does it happen that there are weeds in with the wheat?"

The farmer answered, "An enemy must have sowed the weeds after we sowed the wheat."

"Do you want us to go and pull up the weeds?" the servants asked.

"No, that would never do," answered the farmer, "because in pulling up the weeds you would harm the roots of the wheat. We will have to let both grow until harvest time. Then I will tell those who reap the wheat, 'Cut down the weeds first and bind them in bundles to be burned, but gather the wheat into my barn where it will be safe and ready to be made into flour and bread'."

Thus Jesus taught that a time will come when God will separate the evil from the good, but that time will be in the next world, not in this world.

PARABLE 11

Man's Best Friend

This story takes us back across thousands of years to a beautiful place called "The Garden of Eden." It was there, you remember, that God placed the first man and woman, known to us as Adam and Eve.

The man and his wife were commanded to take care of the garden and were told that they might freely eat of the fruit of all the trees that grew there, except one. God also gave to Adam the responsibility of naming the animals and the birds.

One of the animals, to whom Adam had given the Hebrew name "Keleb," was more friendly than all the others. Everywhere the man and his wife happened to go, as they cared for the garden, their little four-footed friend might be seen trotting along behind.

One morning Keleb found Adam and Eve sitting near the gate of the garden with their faces buried in their hands. Running to them he whimpered and wagged his tail — his way of asking what was the matter.

Patting him on the head, Adam said, "You are not to blame, my little friend. It's all our fault. You see, when God put my wife and me in this beautiful garden, He told us that the fruit on one of the trees we were not to eat. But we disobeyed Him. So, now we have to leave."

Keleb had a feeling that the man and his wife were not altogether to blame. He was sure it was partly the serpent's fault. He had never cared for the old serpent anyway. And now, for Adam and Eve's sake, he wished he could kill him. He started back through the garden, looking for him.

After a little he found him — at the foot of the tree where he had persuaded Adam and Eve to eat the fruit that God had commanded them not to eat.

Keleb bared his teeth, growled, and made ready to fight, but the wicked serpent turned quickly and slithered into a hole in the ground where Keleb could not follow.

Back to the gate of the garden he hurried and found Adam and Eve just going out. Beside the gate an angel was standing. Keleb dropped his head and started to go out too. But the angel stopped him. "You don't have to leave," he said. "You haven't done anything wrong. You can stay with me and keep on living in the beautiful garden."

Keleb looked up into the angel's face. He wagged his tail, gave a friendly little bark, and said, "But God made me to be their friend. And something tells me they are going to need a friend more than ever in the cold hard world outside the garden. So, if you don't mind, let me go out with them and continue to stay close by them and help them to keep the old serpent away from their door."

The angel turned to Adam and Eve. "I am sure," he said, "that God will be greatly pleased to hear what Keleb has said. Because," he continued, "God feels the same way Himself. Although you have sinned by disobeying God, He still loves you; He is still your Friend; He still wants to stay close beside you and to help you to keep the old serpent (which stands for sin and temptation) away from your door."

Then to Keleb, still waiting hopefully, he said, "Go, little animal, as you have asked.

Man's best friend

Be known henceforth as 'Man's best friend'."

Then the angel allowed Keleb to go out of the garden with the man and his wife, that they might never forget how God loved them.

I trust you will never forget that either, when I tell you that Keleb's Hebrew name translated into English is d-o-g, "dog."

Turn that word around, spell it with capital letters, and what do you have? God's own great, wonderful name — G-O-D!

The Story of the Loving Father
(Luke 15:11-24)

Once upon a time there was a man who had two sons. One day the younger of the two said to his father, "Father, I want my share of the property that belongs to you, at once." His father granted his request.

Not many days later this son sold off everything he had received, gathered up the money, and set out for a distant country.

When he arrived he began wasting his money and having a good time. Almost before he knew it, it was all gone.

Soon after, a great famine swept through the land, and there were times when he had nothing to eat. His new-found friends, who were always around when he had money to spend, were no longer interested in him.

He tramped the streets begging for work, but no jobs were to be had in the city. At last he found a farmer, away out in the country, who agreed to give him the job of tending his hogs.

This farmer sent him into the field with no advance pay, not even a meal. By this time he was so hungry that he was tempted to eat some of the pods and roots that the hogs were eating.

He sat down and began to think. "What a fool I am," he said. "Back home even my father's hired servants have more than enough to eat, and here I am about to starve." He was so homesick that he buried his face in his hands and wept.

Then he said: "I am going back home to my father, and I will say to him, 'Father, I have sinned against God and against you. I don't deserve to be called your son any more. But let me come back and work for you as one of your hired servants'."

So he got up and started back home.

Now his father had never forgotten him. Every day he longed for his son, and many,

many times he would look down the road, hoping to see him coming back.

And so it came to pass that before the son arrived at the door, while he was still far down the road, his father saw him and recognized him, although he was in rags. Then the father ran to meet him and fell on his neck and kissed him again and again!

Arm in arm they walked toward the house. They were almost to the door before the son found his voice. "Father," he began, "I have sinned against God and against you. I don't deserve to be called your son any more."

But his father would hear none of it. Breaking in, he shouted to the servants, "Quick, bring the best robe and put it on him, and a ring for his finger and shoes for his feet! And run, kill the fattest calf in the herd, that we may have a feast and be happy! For my son is back home! It is as though he were dead and is alive again! He was lost and is found!"

By this story Jesus was teaching that though we may forget God and go far away into sin, He is a loving Father who never ceases to care for us and to long for our return.